Ashley's Easter egg Hunt disaster

By Nianah Forest

Ashley loves eating Easter chocolates and sometimes she eats a bit more than enough. Follow the story of Ashley as she and her friends go on an Easter egg hunt.

Copyright©. All rights reserved. No part of this book can be reproduced without Owners' Permission.

ISBN:978-1-916554-06-1

This is me Ashley

Funny book about Easter Egg Hunt for children age 2 - 7 years

Once upon a time, there was a young girl named Ashley who greatly adored Easter chocolate eggs.

She loved them so much that every year she would ask her parents to buy her as many as possible. And every year, without fail, she would eat them all in one go.

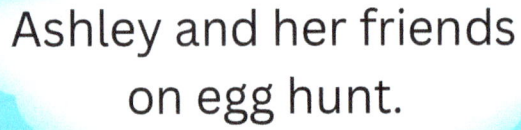

Ashley and her friends on egg hunt.

This year, Ashley's parents had given her a large basket of chocolate eggs, and she had eaten every single one of them. But little did she know that her love for chocolate would have some unexpected results.

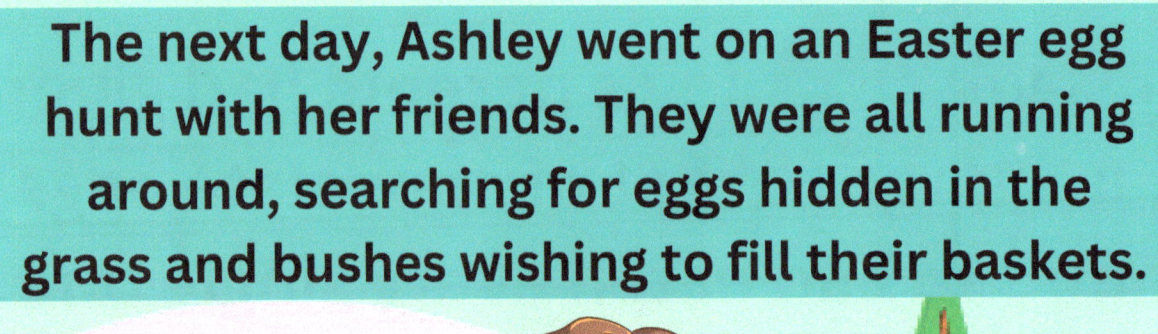

The next day, Ashley went on an Easter egg hunt with her friends. They were all running around, searching for eggs hidden in the grass and bushes wishing to fill their baskets.

But every time Ashley leaned to pick up an egg, she let out a loud fart and shouted oh!

At first, Ashley's friends giggled and laughed, thinking it was just a one-time thing. But as they continued the egg hunt, Ashley kept farting every time.

It got to the point where her friends were starting to avoid her, holding their noses and starring at her with not so kind faces.

Ashley felt so embarrassed and ashamed. She had never experienced anything like this before. She tried to hold it in, but it was no use. It just kept coming out, loud and smelly.

After the egg hunt was over, Ashley went home feeling unhappy. She knew that eating too much chocolate eggs was to blame for her embarrassing problem. From that day on, she made a promise to herself to never eat too much chocolate again.

Although Ashley's friends made fun of her that day, they soon forgave her and forgot about the incident. And Ashley learned a valuable lesson about the consequences of eating too much, both for herself and those around her.

Over the next few days, Ashley avoided her friends and felt ashamed about what had happened on the Easter egg hunt. She didn't want to face them again, knowing that they would just laugh and make fun of her.

But one day, Ashley's mother sat her down for a talk. She explained to her that it was okay to make mistakes, and that everyone has moments they're not proud of. She told her that it was important to learn from her mistakes and move forward, instead of dwelling on them and feeling ashamed and unhappy.

Ashley realized that her mother was right. She had made a mistake by eating too much chocolate, and she had learned an important lesson from it. She decided to apologize to her friends and explain what had happened, hoping that they would understand.

To her surprise, Ashley's friends were much more understanding than she had expected. They listened to her explanation and even shared their own embarrassing stories. They told her that they still valued her as a friend, farts and all.

From then on, Ashley was much more aware of what she ate and made sure not to gobble too many sweets. She still loved Easter chocolate eggs, but she learned to enjoy them in moderation.

In the end, Ashley learned that it was important to be honest with herself and others, even if it meant admitting to embarrassing mistakes.

She also learned that true friends will always stick by you, no matter what. And most importantly, she learned to listen to her body and take care of herself all the time.

Listening to your body is an important aspect of self-care.

Listen to your body, respond to its signals, and take action to maintain good health everyday.

www.ingramcontent.com/pod-product-compliance
Lightning Source LLC
Chambersburg PA
CBHW051323110526
44590CB00031B/4448